# *Remote Work Rockstar*

*How to work and lead successfully
in a virtual environment.*

**by Debbie Lundberg with Barb Zant**

How to work and lead successfully in a virtual environment.

Copyright 2020
by Presenting Powerfully by Debbie Lundberg
4621 W. Bay to Bay Blvd.
Tampa, FL 33629

ISBN: 978-0-578-68640-0

First Edition.

This material has been written and published solely for educational purposes. The author shall have neither liability nor responsibility to any person or entity with respect to any loss, damage or injury caused or alleged to be caused directly or indirectly by the information contained in this book.

Edited by Betsey Hapner, Esq.

Book cover design by Sue Nance.

# *Remote Work Rockstar*

## *How to work and lead successfully in a virtual environment.*

### *by Debbie Lundberg with Barb Zant*

3

*With special thanks to friends, family, colleagues, workshop attendees, and clients, who knowingly or not, contributed to the learning and sharing of being a ROCKSTAR when working remotely, and therefore, contributed to this book!*

## *Contents*

# Introduction

# Closing Comments

# Introduction

Thank you for wanting to enhance and improve your life in the area of remote work!

Here we are in 2020, and many have been experiencing remote work themselves, as leaders of remote workers, or both. How many, though, feel as if they can claim their efforts as "Rockstar" when it comes to working remotely?

If you find yourself embracing being out of the office, challenged to adapt to working outside the office, you thought that remote work would be short term, or even if you are considering leading a remote team, *then this book is for you.*

The vast world of being viral is growing, and it is my desire for you to grow, prosper and shine on that remote stage!

Since there are norms that develop in environments (in person or otherwise), ensure your Virtual Work Etiquette is a "Do" and not a "Don't."

And, while the foundational efforts will absolutely be covered, this book is less about simply conducting work remotely, this book is about rockin' it – this is about being a *Remote Work Rockstar*!

And, as I explore, define, or even defend choosing the word Rockstar, please know that the vision of a Rockstar is that of someone who presents professionally, feels confident, and has both pride and humility in efforts…whether with others in the same space, across miles or across the internet.

Here are some other titles that I first considered before landing on "Remote Work Rockstar": Leading Successfully in a Remote Economy, Leading Well in a Virtual Economy, Remote Work

Success, Be Virtually Present, Success in a Virtual Economy, Working Smart – Working Remotely, Being Relevant While Being Virtual, Relevant Rockstar, and How to Become a Remote Work Rockstar.

You see, that is where a discussion with Barb came in, and that is how I invited her to contribute a few ideas and perspective to this book. When I asked her, she quickly, and excitedly agreed to allow me to ask her some questions and run a few things past her. With gratitude for listening to my gut to ask to hear her thoughts, I am thrilled with the outcome, and importantly, hopefully, you are, too!

A little bit of background...

Barb and I met over a decade ago when Barb was a client of my Consulting and Executive Presence Coaching service. My company, Presenting Powerfully, had a yearly "subscription" offer that included one-on-one coaching, and entre into a group focused on personal and professional development. That group, known as Leading Ladies of Learning, collaborated to receive mentoring, coaching and to develop confidence in public speaking and sales presentation skill. They were female executives, leaders, and aspiring leaders from various industries. Barb was a Leading Lady of Learning for eight of the ten years that the invitation-only supportive experience existed. In December of 2018, the group was redirected to an online platform for continued sharing, as together, we started something new to keep the inspiration, challenge, and learning going, as we discovered we shared some common goals.

Our next step together was to launch a podcast. Our vision for that venture, the publishing of a consistently upbeat, realistic 20-minutes-or-less per episode show, was to inspire listeners to continue to be people embracing every chance to accomplish and experience all they can…in business and life. The Business of Life Masterclass Podcast was born (TBOL) in October 2018, and launched fully in May 2019 with multiple episodes for binge listening.

On each of our interview shows, we ask the "podcast 4" questions (as we call them), and wow, the guests have given us such terrific answers, and still do! We supplement and complement each episode with a "follow-through" show, where Barb and I share what we implemented based on the guest's ideas, and how that went. We have had a lot of opportunities to challenge our thoughts and actions through the process…and we still do.

The content from the podcast is evolving to include coaching, strategy sessions, workshops and multiple day conferences where we share and invite former show guest to offer more than they could in the brief, high-energy recording of their segment.

Then came COVID-19.

Life, as we knew it, changed.

I worked remotely for my entire (nearly)14-year practice, and much of my time with General Motors and Dale Carnegie Training. In fact, I delivered talks and webinars on the topic of Remote Work Success as part of my practice for over a decade, so (thankfully), my knowledge and sharing fast became a community resource in early 2020.

As the typical in-office workforce became remote workers overnight, many scrambled to put together an office space quickly. It became apparent that long-lasting change to how we worked would propel all of us into the future. Working remotely was not just a passing trend, or burden, or luxury, depending on your vantage point, for only a few.

As I continued to see both successes and mistakes being made, the demand for even more remote work content was immediate. After all, remote work success is quite different than remote work survival. It is more than opening a Zoom account and having meetings via video. The idea for this book was readily requested, and while the first thoughts were that the idea was flattering, quickly that concept turned into what you now hold in your hands.

Keeping in mind that little stands true in our more traditional work that does not apply to the virtual environment, the aim of this publication is to bridge our traditional work success with the idiosyncrasies of the remote work environment in order to serve as a guidebook and, I dare claim it as a "behind-the-scenes coach" for whomever is interested and willing to make changes to get to Rockstar status.

This book has seven chapters. There will be guidelines/suggestions and a mention or a story of what has really happened along the way. It is not just based in theory; as a matter of fact, there is little theory, rather, you will find implementable tactics suggested that are based on multiple experiences.

At the end of each chapter, since some of you are reading this as a leader of remote workers, or someone who aspires to be, a few Remote Work Rockstar Leadership Tips (RWRLT) are disclosed as they are shared in a bulleted format for a concise close to the material on that chapter's subject matter. The intentional titles and content of the chapters were born from experience in the virtual world where I have lived and worked for a long time, and where Barb found herself thrust.

As briefly shared earlier, I wrote this book based on my speaking engagements, and invited Barb to offer her input and perspective as her experiences were different than mine. I really appreciate having her "with me" offering some contributions to this publication!

Thank you again for allowing these guidelines to clear up any questions you might have on your mind for remote work success.

After all, while each of us may not see everyone a lot, often, or you may see them only as an image on a screen or screen name, each person deserves respect and consideration.

Please be engaged, get active, and stay energized as you are about to embark on this phase of your journey to becoming a **Remote Work Rockstar**!

Cheers to your success,

*Debbie Lundberg*

# Chapter 1:
## Defining Remote Work

*"We like to give people the freedom to work where they want, safe in the knowledge that they have the drive and expertise to perform excellently, whether they at their desk or in their kitchen. Yours truly has never worked out of an office, and never will."*

*~ Sir Richard Branson,*

*Virgin America*

Defining remote work may seem like something very simple, and yet it is not. It is not simple because people have complicated the concept with misperceptions over the years.

The term "remote work" is intentionally used in this book as the type of work that is completed away from an office or from an entity's headquarters or regional location. Other words or terms that are appropriate to use include: off-site work, virtual work, tele-work, and the phrase "working remotely".

*Phrases such as "working from home", "work from home", or "home at work" are not recommended.*

The reason "remote work" is used is because it includes the concept of work that is being done, along with the idea that it is done off-site or remotely. When phrases such as "work from home" are used, it introduces the idea of being at home and doing things that we typically do in our house or home while merely attempting to co-mingle or fit in our work.

Respecting this may seem like semantics, and, to a certain degree, it is, at the same time, remote work keeps the emphasis on the work and the fact that we are being respectful of the work being done. This way, all of us are avoiding that implication that we think someone is doing things at home, and happens to be including some work along the way!

It may strike you as unfortunate that I start the book with defining the foundation for the writing in terms of terminology based on what this type of off-site employee faces. And yet, it is necessary, for this is the beginning of a shift about, *and for*, the success of a remote worker. This movement toward respecting and positioning remote work includes the mindful act of not asking someone "Do you work from home?", but rather asking "Do you work remotely?" Shifting habits such as language shares a perspective, and appreciation, so to speak, for the fact that employment, or entrepreneurialism, regardless of the location, is still about the work being performed.

Remote work can be a permanent part of a job description, can be a temporary part of an assignment for a particular team or project, or can be a reward for people who prefer it. How you introduce remote work to an environment matters. For example, back to the language, I have experienced companies saying "We know a lot of people want to work from home because it's easier . . . " Saying something like that does not imply respect for remote work, instead it makes it sound as though there is a belief that people are working less, and certainly at a different pace, if they are not on location, with oversight leaders. Also, if people are forced to work remotely, such as in the COVID-19 pandemic, a lot of people do not have the tools, plan in place, and the discipline, to have success. That does not mean they do not *want* to have the tools, discipline, and success; rather it means it is not necessarily natural to them…or been afforded to them.

*That brings me to whether or not remote work is for everyone.*

If you did experience any conversations about remote work in the recent past, and it would be surprising if you had not, and you had an interest in this book, it may be because many people talked at length about their dislike for remote work.

It is my hypothesis that remote work can be as productive, or more productive, as on-site work, for the right temperament, conditions, and expectations. Nearly anyone put in a remote work environment without the proper positioning and support, will minimally have missteps, and likely, have failures, and therefore may seem as though they are not suited for remote work.

Am I saying everyone is suited for remote work? *No, I am not.* However, please believe that nearly everyone can function successfully when working remotely, if given the opportunity to appreciate how remote workflow and the expectations of a remote worker are anticipated at the onset (or as soon as you finish this book).

Now that it is clear that this is not a "I have to work from home" book, and remote work has been defined as being many things, depending on the circumstance, let's move forward with the tactics and application necessary to generate a remote workforce that feels included, important, and like a contributing factor in the success of the business ahead.

During COVID-19, Barb was suddenly a remote worker and, on top of that, she was expected to be a remote leader…with no warning and certainly no training!

During the first week that her team was working remote, they stumbled, and were even dumbfounded thinking it would be a lot more fun because it would be a lot less work. Heck, they were even calling it "work from home". Instead, it became apparent that it was much like working in an office, as it should have been.

Most of the mistakes made will have been detailed in the following chapters with no direct call outs to the when or the who, as they are for reference and not ridicule!

Everything from not have a proper office set up or technology to not having expectations set transpired, and quickly became DON'Ts in a world where they used to know what to DO.

Their schedules and habits were off. At first, they connected only by phone. And, their personal schedules (virtual classroom and workouts) bled into the workday, so being virtually visible seemed nearly impossible – and forget about a professional image! As a matter of fact, dressing for the day, and, oh boy, even showering, seemed optional to everyone from the newest team member to the most senior of sales leader as they entered a new time for them all. They had a lot to learn. With millions of dollars in sales at stake, it was fortunate they were fast learners!

With that in mind, here is the first set of Remote Work Rockstar Leadership Tips:

**RWRLT** Use the terms "Remote Work", and "Working Remotely" in all communication regarding off-site engagements and employees.

**RWRLT** Include remote workers in all meetings that you would have that you would have invited them to be a part of if they were on site.

▪RWRLT▪ When on-boarding remote workers, ensure that they are able to come on site and meet people, if on site is not possible, have a video on-boarding process/experience that is interactive, *not recorded.*

▪RWRLT▪ In each meeting where there is a remote worker, include video, and if there is a failure in the video, put a name tent with that person's identification (name and title with a photo, if possible) on it next to the speaker phone that is being used, as this will assist in not forgetting that person is on the line, and who that person is.

▪RWRLT▪ Ensure that people who are working remotely are included in any incentives and events.

▪RWRLT▪ Have biographies for every one of your employees, regardless of their position, with a photo that is current, so that everybody can see each other.

▪RWRLT▪ Feature two individuals (or more) each month for the organization – one who is on site, and at least one who is remote, so people get to know colleagues and co-workers through the ideas shared in that feature.

`RWRLT` Choose the words that define remote work for your organization and stick with them, and then utilize the vocabulary you choose to communicate remote work on an ongoing basis with consistency.

`RWRLT` Remember that people who choose to do some work at night off-site, after work at home or on the weekends, when they typically work in the office, *are not the same as remote workers.* Stay true to how remote work is defined for your teams, especially if some of your team members switch back and forth from remote work and office work for projects and/or assignments.

Defining "remote work" is complete. And, you know that Remote Work Rockstars not only embrace their role, they are memorable for their performance as a contributor, and not as someone who is *that* man or woman who never comes into the office!

# Chapter 2:
# Getting Set Up Remotely

*"Don't work from bed. You want your bed to be a place of peace and calm, not work stress."*

*~ Liz Grossman Kitoyi,*
*Baobab Consulting*

While a lot of preparation can be made to ready oneself for remote work, there can also be situations that dictate a swift change.

As there are many options for how you may choose to telework, the Remote Work Rockstar would ideally have the following (stay with me, as this is the very long IDEAL list, and, the much shorter realistic set-up strategy list will follow):

☆ A room with a door that can be closed, to call an office and use solely as an office to keep work separate from the rest of the living space where you are.
☆ A desk with the option of standing or sitting for variety in body positioning and perspective.
☆ An ergonomic desk chair for body support and comfort.
☆ A laptop with a good camera and adequate storage.
☆ Multiple screens for use with various programs.
☆ A visible, accurate clock.
☆ A timer.

☆ A strong Wi-Fi connection for multiple devices being consistently connected.

☆ Adequate lighting, including natural light in the room (not direct sunlight behind you) and a bright light behind the laptop or desktop being used for videoconferencing (it'll highlight expressions and keep the fellow videoconferencers seeing a face versus shadows or darkness).

☆ Many notepads and pens for "listening through writing", meaning as people see note-taking, they sense a respect for the engagement.

☆ Noise-canceling headphones for phone and video sessions. Still, be aware that noise-cancelling headphones keep the noise out of the wearer's head, and yet when off mute, the noise-cancelling headphones still only cancel out that internally, and externally, if there are noises in the space, other people on the call or in the video meeting will hear that.

☆ A consistent, useful, personality-pleasing calendaring system for keeping meetings in order and all in one place. Resist keeping plans all over in various formats, as something will get forgotten or overlooked.

☆ A coffee maker and fridge for snacks and staying on a sound health plan.

☆ A whiteboard and/or a chalkboard for tracking projects, projects, and for using during video conferences for noting items of interests, commitments and more.

☆ At least one filing cabinet for keeping items out of the way and staying on top of clients, customers, orders, and other business-related items.

☆ An organization system that is something other than sticky notes or piles, and a process that fits your style and approach so that you will use it fully and not see it as an inconvenience.

☆ A color printer for documents to share with others.

☆ A high-volume printer that may be black and white for less-formal documents and drafts to proof.

☆ Paper for printing quickly from the remote site.

☆ Plants for energy in the room.
☆ A photo or two of people or a place that brings joy.
☆ An inspiring, calming element, such as a water feature or sound machine for a calm background/backdrop with peaceful energy.
☆ A fan for cooling the room (not to be on during a video session or meeting, as it chops up the light).
☆ Glasses with blue-light cancellation if you wear glasses.

Whew! That is a lot, isn't it? Those are over 20 ideas for having the ideal Remote Work Rockstar set-up – and that list may not even be complete. It is exhaustive as of this book's writing, and yet it could, and likely will, grow!

Respecting that list includes everything that would be *ideal*, and perhaps something to target over time, regardless of how long you will be working remotely, you minimally want what is deemed as the realistic (the minimum) for an effective life as a

Remote Work Rockstar, and they include the following four contributors for RWR necessities:

☆ A dedicated space. While the best scenario is that room with a locking door, we respect that may not be "in the cards" for everyone. To dedicate space, here is what that may look like:

  ☆ A desk set up in a room that is shared with another purpose.

  ☆ A desk built into a nook or attached space in the kitchen.

  ☆ A table in place of a desk for teleworking.

  ☆ A portion of a table that is taped off (yes, really tape it off) or divided for work and something else.

  ☆ A card table that is set up and taken down at various times due to space-sharing.

These last two are the least desired of scenarios, as it really is meant as *dedicated space,* and while the table may be the only things dedicated, it is better than working "wherever you can on whatever day", so they are included as options. Often when working with clients, they share that these choices were not even considered, and yet with a table for work during work, there can still be a sense of dedicated workspace. (How to "close the door" on these alternates to a full office will be addressed in a later chapter.)

☆ Comfort is key. This is not about lounging, rather that the dedicated space is not configured for physical discomfort. In other words, using a child's desk is not an option, and/or having your head hit a cupboard if you lean in to adjust your laptop's camera position will not work long-term, either. Cushions, tidying the space around you (including at your feet), and making the area "yours" will be instrumental in your desire to be in the space, and while you are there, being productive!

☆ A device that has phone and internet access, some space for apps and storage, and a working camera.

☆ This area is to be called your office or workspace, and not the computer room or something else that is not related to your work or office. Even if small or seemingly contrived, the area is now your space for remote work, so naming it that, seeing it as that, and communicating that, even if only to yourself, is the way to embrace it as the spot where you get work accomplished, and that will assist you in being disciplined in the virtual and remote environment.

Being invited to deliver talks on remote work used to be something that happened occasionally.

When remote work became much more mainstream in 2020, talks on what to do and not do became instant hits for companies to offer.

While I would send a video and one-pager ahead of time for people to be prepared for the session, inevitably something strange would happen. People would name the meeting a Zoom Call or Teams Call, so people thought it was a phone call. In the first 10 sessions of delivering the talk "Working Effectively When Working Remotely", amazingly, there were over 45 cameras that, according to the "callers" did not work, and there were 22 people who were outside with noises around them that kept them from hearing the presentation, and sunshine that kept them from seeing it. There were people smoking and eating full meals during the video sessions. Would you ever dream of smoking or eating an entire meal while in an in-person meeting? If the answer is "no", and I hope it is, then don't excuse that behavior because you are off-site!

It was a clear case (collectively) of many people not being set up for remote work and thinking that winging it with a smart phone at their house was sufficient for their working environment functionality. Yikes!

Surely nobody is perfect, and while redemption can be found/created in the next meeting and the next session, and the next conference when remote, there are those first impressions that become stories, and even legends...and not the ones you want to be a part of in your professional endeavors.

In order to avoid those missteps for your team members, and to let the RWR know you are supporting them from afar, here are some Remote Work Rockstar Leadership Tips:

**RWRLT** Provide a "getting started" kit of basics for the office during on-boarding or when someone moves to remote work from the office. This kit might include scissors, tape, a stapler, some gift cards to a chain for office equipment and more.

**RWRLT** Set aside a budget for Remote Work Rockstars to minimally have the basics.

**RWRLT** Establish a budget for travel for RWRs, ideally, with them, and make sure you share the final budget with them.

**RWRLT** Provide an efficient way for supplies to be ordered without a delay in approval or reimbursement.

**RWRLT** Ask for a photo/selfie from each of your team in their remote workspace to show you care about their environment. Share them out in a fun way that shows the personalities of your RWRs.

**RWRLT** Have incentives that drive behaviors for enhancing the remote work office or workspace.

**RWRLT** Share photos and articles on successful remote work environments.

**RWRLT** Include a portion of your update, newsletter or town hall meeting be dedicated to remote work updates and successes.

**RWRLT** Consider contests for efficiency-sharing and best-practice teachings among your team – remote and otherwise to encourage sharing and collaboration.

**RWRLT** Send handwritten notes to each of your team members. In that message, ensure they know you want them to have all they need to be successful.

**RWRLT** Set the standard with your own set up. Rock it. Be virtually visible regularly during the hours you have set with them for access to you.

**RWRLT** Schedule a video conference with your team and/or individuals to see for yourself how they are doing and how they sound (literally). Read body language. Collaborate with them regarding what is still needed so you can inspire, connect, and encourage their confidence in being a Remote Work Rockstar.

**RWRLT**   Have your team members lead daily meetings so they can become comfortable with sharing their screen and showing presentations with video. Get a professional, if you are not an expert, as you do not want to take for granted that they know how to do this (or that you do).

**RWRLT**   Have your Information Technology department available. Most issues can be figured out quickly with little stress when expertise is utilized.

**RWRLT**   Ensure training on new tools, even beyond presenting, is provided for them to gain skills and for the team feel supported.

Being successfully set up for remote work is essential. The set up process is the difference in just making it work and really *working it*!

Both Remote Work Rockstars and RWR Leaders can be cognizant of how the environment impacts productivity and connectivity as you all strive to achieve goals together…even if minutes or miles separate you!

# Chapter 3:
# Setting Expectations & Establishing Habits

*"Telecommuting, one of many forms of work-life flexibility, should no longer be viewed as a nice-to-have, optional perk mostly used by working moms. These common stereotypes don't match reality—allowing employees to work remotely is a core business strategy today... We need to de-parent, de-gender, and de-age the perception of the flexible worker."*

*~ Cali Williams Yost,*

*Flex+Strategy Group & Work+Life Fit*

Not surprisingly, many people transition to remote work without any discussion about the change, questions, concerns, or expectations.

Sometimes the change is as swift as being in the office on a Friday and starting remotely on the following Monday.

*I absolutely don't recommend that!*

Oddly, there tend to be a few beliefs that can play out, including "You're lucky – you don't have to come into the office" so there is some resentment toward the remote worker, or "No news is good news", whereas people forget about those off-site, or "Now that you're working remotely, you have to be available 24 hours a day, 7 days a week, or else someone might think you are not working hard enough, or at all", and that is not something that can be maintained, nor should it!

Regardless of how you have felt in the past, clear expectation-setting, coupled with establishing well-serving habits, are both imperative for the success of remote work. Together, these actions establish boundaries, and boundaries are types of "rules of the road" for people on both sides of this remote work journey!

Let's start with expectations.

Expectations are three-pronged, including: 1) what can be expected from the supervisor/manager/leader, 2) what can be expected from the off-site employee, and 3) what can be expected from the rest of the team or company.

Expectation-setting starts with a conversation, and while communication is the topic of chapter

5, there are a few tips shared here to get the juices flowing, and the process starter.

Be careful, as there can be actions that seem like micromanagement and others that feel like "sink or swim" when working remotely. To avoid that, as a Remote Work Rockstar, or RWR in-process, first, discuss the following with your leader(s):

☆ Preferred ways to communicate. You have yours, and your leader has his or hers. Talk through them and establish what is best for the two of you, or the group of you. Positively determine that if there is an emergency, what is the protocol for communication.

☆ How your work fits into the group work, the location work, and the company overall (your part in the success of the organization).

☆ Who sets prioritization if/when others have requests of you.

☆ The dynamic of other team members and/or leaders in the group, and that impact on your work/role.

☆ What, specifically, are your typical/standard working hours.

☆ When and how to communicate/discuss changes in plans or deadlines.

☆ How you like to receive recognition.

☆ The personal and professional goals you have. Yes, both personal and professional goal-setting and goal-sharing play well into establishing expectations, and therefore, boundaries, too.

☆ Paid Time Off (PTO) rules and processes, along with vacations that are planned. Additionally, what expectations are appropriate when on vacation. Are there points of contact, no engagement? What is anticipated must be covered.

☆ Education, training, and/or schooling goals you have established and/or plan to complete.

☆ Frequency of updates. What is too much, versus what makes it seem like you are not reachable or engaged means having a talk about establishing check-ins and formal updates, too.

☆ How the team perceives your role.

☆ How often you'll be included in on-site meetings.

☆ Responsibilities, accountability and authority. These three are the triad of accomplishment. If any are not aligned, miscommunication, and therefore, misdirection will almost inevitably follow.

Once you have expectations set for your role and that of what is fair to expect from your leader and your team members, you have a solid footing for moving forward successfully while teleworking.

Still, you are alone, for a lot of the day, at least when it comes to being around colleagues and co-workers. That can create wonderful opportunities for productivity, huge distractions for lack of productivity, or both! Habits that are well-serving to a Remote Work Rockstar are tremendously important. Discipline is ingrained in many of us from the way we were raised, and yet in a remote work environment, even the most dedicated of personalities and temperaments can be tempted to "go down a rabbit hole" and get off track quickly and often!

To avoid that, here are some proven habits, both simple and complex to consider implementing. Here are the simple:

☆ Keep your traditional sleep schedule. Even though you may have previously had commute time, and you can sleep longer or differently, unless you were lacking sleep, keep your sleep pattern remarkably close to when you work in a traditional office environment. If you vary it, start with staying within an hour of your bedtime and wake time in order to give your body and mind the knowledge, so to speak, that there will be rest.

☆ Stay true to routine as much as possible. Similar to your sleep schedule, routines are not meant to restrict, rather routines tend to regulate, and regulated behaviors allow for mental and physical ease, where stress is minimized. A tweak to a routine, such as adding in movement/exercise during what used to be a commute time will serve as a new habit and change the routine in action and not time spent, so that change may lead to improvements in physical activity and eventually, productivity.

☆ Have office hours. As non-remote workers do, have times that you go to work. One of the best things about remote work is that it is always there, and one of the worst things about remote work is that it is always there. So, set a schedule to arrive at work and to end your workday. Having a door, as mentioned in Chapter 2, can assist in this effort through the act of opening and closing that door for office work.

☆ Set alarms for most everything, meaning each day, when reviewing your calendar, set alarms a couple of minutes prior to calls and video conferences to ensure you do not get "in too deep" and overlook the start of a meeting or call.

☆ Communicate your daily schedule w/others in your space. You may work in a house, apartment, or townhouse/condominium, or in a shared workspace, or a communal area with dedicated workspace. There will inevitably (or quickly) be annoyances such as interruptions, or worse yet, embarrassments, of inappropriate intrusions. These will happen, and yet they can be avoided for the most part by minimally communicating a visual schedule or verbal sharing each day of what is happening when (video conferences and phone calls, in particular). Having a "Meeting in Progress" sign on your door or at your space can reinforce what is happening at certain times. If you are in your house and children are present, having them create a decorative sign for you keeps them involved and they become part of the process for communicating "meeting time" through the sign they make.

☆ Take breaks. Remote workers often find their posture suffers, and even their digestion can be impacted if they do not honor their bodily need for movement and stretching. Minimally, get up each hour for a physical break. If you do not naturally do that, or your watch is not programmed to remind you, set a timer. This is not silly, this is essential.

Those implementations of new habits, or reinforcement of existing actions are what I call "simple". Simple and easy are not synonymous, so if you feel as though those are enough. Stop there and make them happen for you, intentionally, and mindfully, first.

When you are ready, here are some more complex habits to embrace in concept and then implement through practice:

☆ Shower, dress & be "ready" for work each day. Remote workers who think of their role as "work from home" fall prey to the idea of loungewear is appropriate, and it's often noted that those who wear their slippers all day are less productive than those with shoes on. Strangely, or perhaps it's logical, that when we are in work attire, we are in work mode, and therefore, we get work accomplished.

☆ Eat "healthily" for you. Snacking can be convenient. Heck, it was suggested in Chapter 2 that both a coffee maker and refrigerator in your office would be ideal! Still, you know your body best, watch what you are feeding your work machine, as you want to feel good and productive, rather than sloppy and sluggish.

☆ Move your body. While this may look like a repeat of the simple bullet above that suggested you take breaks, this goes deeper. Moving your body, meaning walking, running, dancing, or whatever fits for your interests, is something needed to replace the steps you would have been taking in an office or site where trips to restrooms, meetings and even the cafeteria or breakroom, added up over the course of the day. Stagnation is a silent drainer of the remote worker, so Remote Work Rockstars move it!

☆ Practice gratitude. Sometimes people find this a strange strategy to recommended habits, and yet I passionately believe this is essential to remote work success for the Remote Work Rockstar. The reason practicing gratitude is part of a good routine when teleworking is similar to the lift it gives anyone in that thinking, saying and writing down something, someone or some opportunity for which you are grateful puts you in the mindset of gratitude (more to follow in Chapter 4), and that creates positive energy and perspective. No matter how isolated or empowered you feel working off-site, you can control your attitude, and an attitude of gratitude is one to embrace. It is recommended that you record your "grateful gets", which are people, experiences or thoughts you got to experience, either first thing in the morning or last thing at night (or both).

☆ No venting on social media about your remote work or your company. Those rants rarely make you look professional, and without the context of people being around you, you can look ungrateful and to those at your company, you can seem negative. Address issues with people directly, and policy challenges with your leadership to keep social media for the social side of life.

☆ If you do vent to a colleague or friend or family member, set a time limit on it. Really, set a timer of 2-5 minutes, and then move on!

☆ Journal. Keeping thoughts in order, on paper, or in an electronic journal can assist in keeping things from getting away from you. Journaling varies from gratitude in that any, and all thoughts are to be indulged in a journal – disappointments, ideas, creativity, non-work thoughts. It serves as a form of an outlet for maintaining harmony in life. (Notice I don't use the term "balance"? There is no "work-life balance" section to this chapter, or even the book, as it is not about teetering on a wire to have balance that is delicately mastered, rather Remote Work Rockstars harmonize each aspect of life.) Sometimes work is front and center, and other times family is. When we strive for harmony, they play together well, where often balance feels like a chore that never ends!

☆ Keep your sense of humor muscles exercised. Remote work has its own benefits and quirky moments, so much like there are oddities that happen in an office, there will be funny things that happen in your remote office space. You may have a cat attempt to get on your keyboard or a dog wanting to bark during a call or meeting, or you may simply misinterpret something or someone. Having the desire and ability to move past some of these hiccups often takes a sense of humor and a belief that there are funny moments provided in life to bring ease at times where it is needed!

Similar to how expectations and habits are key for the Remote Work Rockstar to shine, there are many Remote Work Rockstar Leadership tips for guiding and nurturing discipline, too. They include:

**RWRLT** Let people know you care. Do not complain about someone working remotely or ignore a situation simply because someone is remote and not "popping in" your office to get your attention.

**RWRLT** Get and stay positive in tone and energy. That one phone call or video session with your remote worker or team, may come when you just finished a challenging call or meeting, and yet your time with the Remote Work Rockstars is limited, so watch that impression that they may feel as though you are inconvenienced by them.

**RWRLT** Listen to worker's concerns. This may sound like the earlier care tip, and yet it goes beyond letting them know, true listening shows them. *Make sure you really hear what they are saying and what is not being said!*

`RWRLT` Pay attention to the time of your communication and that of your Remote Work Rockstars so that it does not get implied that 24/7 is expected. You can schedule emails for later or the next day, depending on when you are crafting them, and/or you can acknowledge if you are sending something at an unusual time by adding a mention of when a reply is expected (during working hours), you acknowledge and respect that your timeframe of sending is not to impact their response time.

`RWRLT` Encourage self-care for your Remote Work Rockstars. This is true for all teams, remote or not, that a leader who wants each person to tend to what is important for him or her, is a leader who is genuinely engaged and interested. Watch asking too many personal questions yet be sincere in wanting your RWRs to be at their best through self-care such as rest, massage, exercise, or any (legal) stress-relief that works for them.

59

`RWRLT` Offer SLACK or Monday.com (not endorsements of these products in particular), or some form of casual and formal group messaging. Text can suffice if the group/team is small. It is part of connecting, so ensure something is provided that the team, collectively, likes and will use.

`RWRLT` Practice empathy. Much like on-site workers, people join companies and leave managers. Your ability to have an interest in considering your Remote Work Rockstar's perspective and position, means you will be relatable and interested. Empathy is not sympathy, so this is not about feeling sorry for anyone, rather this is about feeling as though you are aware of exemptions and situations and acting accordingly.

`RWRLT` Share your RWRs Human Resources contacts and how to utilize those experts. If you have an Employee Assistance Program, make certain your remote team knows about it and how to access it.

`RWRLT` Resist telling someone it "costs too much" to include that RWR in a meeting, as it devalues that person's contribution.

`RWRLT` Consider themes for events and activities that RWRs can participate in via video.

`RWRLT` Communicate early and often. Remote workers feel left out of meetings and announcements, so ensure they are in the loop, and there are not times when they are the only people left out of a message. Ask if RWRs want to know about birthday and anniversary celebrations, as some do so they can wish that person well even if they will not be there for the cake. Too often, RWRs are removed from communications like those, and the leader thinks it is considerate, when the remote contributors may want to be aware of what is happening. The communication tips expand greatly in Chapter 5.

`RWRLT` Establish one-on-one meeting schedules with each RWR, and don't cancel them, rather, if something gets in the way that is unavoidable, reschedule within the same week.

**RWRLT** Be fair and do not treat everyone the same. Sameness means a lack of empathy and emotional intelligence. Meeting people where they are, rather than treating them like one of many of the same, means you will build trust.

**RWRLT** Clearly communicate work hours should the workload increase. If you expect them to be available off hours, let them know. On the flip side, it can be common for work to blend into family time. Encourage the team to take mental breaks and shut down for the day when the workday is over.

**RWRLT** Being virtually ready means being "dressed" for the workday. Daily morning video meetings will assist the team in seeing that as they set priorities and feel connected.

**RWRLT** Send a video greeting on Monday mornings to inspire, and for the RWRs to feel connected, stay up to date on current information and set weekly priorities.

RWRLT   Be fully transparent and explain the reason behind changes whether perceived as positive or negative.

RWRLT   Support habits that serve the organization and employee well even if they don't appear traditional. Perhaps someone reading in a classroom or mentoring is not typically done, and yet the support of a leader makes the work enjoyable before and after the reading.

RWRLT   Provide ongoing training on establishing habits to support redirection when needed.

RWRLT   Share positive examples of habits that have served your team well.

RWRLT   Encourage working hours that support positive habits.

RWRLT   Celebrate milestones and birthdays with healthy options as an alternative to cake or alcohol.

RWRLT   Champion contests for jokes and stories to share via video so as to include RWR images and ideas with the rest of the organization. Doing this will encourage others to recognize that they, the RWRs, are a big part of the success of the team and the company!

**RWRLT** Lead by example. Remember, you could be working with your RWR, or for your RWR, at some point, so stay a leader of people, and not just a manager of process.

While this may be the longest chapter, it is foundational to have solid expectations and habits for growing as a person and for growing as a team and an organization as well.

The tips mentioned here are detailed, and yet it is the depth of plan that sets the tone for disciplined delivery and a trusting rapport for the Remote Work Rockstar!

# Chapter 4:
# Mastering Mindset

*"People today really value workplace flexibility and remote work because it allows them to focus their energies on work and life as opposed to commuting or other complications due to geography."*
*~ Ken Matos,*
*Life Meets Work*

Mindset may first strike you as a bit "woo-woo" for a business book, and yet it is not something I'd ever want to overlook in this Remote Work Rockstar book.

It's absolutely alright if you gloss over at first, if you race to this section, or you simply take it in stride, as part of the RWR success comes from being different.

So, what is a Remote Work Rockstar mindset? A RWR mindset is one of "Can do", and it is one of "Let's go", and "Bring it on", and yet it is not one of "It's all on me" or "I have to do this alone", or "My team is not a team, so who is going to handle this if I don't handle it".

While those last couple of thoughts of being isolated or working alone, may, unfortunately, be on the minds and in the hearts of many remote workers who don't have Rockstar leaders in their organization, the Remote Work

Rockstar has the mindset of a ROCKSTAR, meaning you are:

- R – Realistically setting and accepting expectations
- O – Opening your approach to collaboration
- C – Checking in on time, resources and progress
- K – Keeping focused on what is best, and not just being right
- S – Setting incremental hurdles to overcome en route to the bigger win
- T – Talking with others (not just "to" others about the what, how, when and who on projects)
- A – Accounting for each person's commitment, and especially your own
- R – Reflecting on what is going well, what can be improved, and stating gaps and goals

In other words, the mindset of a Remote Work Rockstar is positive and productive, centered, and steadfast. Rockstars know they (you) can accomplish much and do not hesitate to call on others to assist or work together.

A few ways to launch and feed a healthy RWR mindset have been mentioned in the comments regarding set up, expectations and habits.

Still, at the risk of slight duplication, a full overview is worth grouping together here in a clear effort to address mindset, and the shifting of mindset should one get feeling off, down, or distracted. This can all be accomplished when you:

☆ Have a personal mantra, brand, tagline or saying that gets you focused in order to be "game on" when working or reestablishing work after a break. Being your best cheerleader means you are self-reliant.

☆ Engage an accountability partner. If that sounds counter to the tip above this one, it is not, rather it is complementary. On goals and objectives, having someone you know and trust to give you support, a push or a push-back if you are not performing, is a solid approach to holding yourself to high standards.

☆ Figure out if music assists or hinders your mood and your productivity. Not all of us are the same. Barb likes music, and I enjoy energy/mood sounds. If there are words, I am sometimes distracted. Sounds are more pleasing to me…the ocean, instruments, or anything calming. Where you gain energy matters, and music and sounds may contribute or distract. Your figuring it out will impact your mindset!

☆ Think and speak in terms of "I want", "I will", "Because", and "I am" instead of thinking in terms of "I have to", or "I need to", or "I should". The first four expressions can be combined into a long statement such as *"I want to deliver a productive, entertaining presentation. I will prepare and rehearse because I am a Remote Work*

*Rockstar!"* This forward-thinking, predictive positive personal positioning greatly impacts mindset and mood! The latter thoughts are burdensome and feel heavy, therefore, they do not support a positive mindset.

☆ Learn to breathe four counts fully in and eight beats out for stabilizing energy when rushed or stressed.

☆ Keep a mirror near your laptop or phone where you take calls and participate in video meetings – check your attitude in the mirror, as we can hear through emails and calls what is on your face. When you use a mirror for awareness and not vanity, you learn a lot about you, too!

☆ Use podcasts, audio books, inspirational talks, quotations, and other go-to feeds of positivity serve as part of your process for engaging in your personal motivation and mindset.

☆ Know what a stress reliever is for you (other than not working for a day while on the clock, or alcohol).

Mindset only goes as far as the environment that it functions in, and here are some Remote Work Rockstar Leadership tips for supporting and promoting that mindset mastery:

RWRLT   Assist with replacing negative words or self-talk with the positive through encouragement and not criticism.

RWRLT   Provide an environment of thinking big and ideation, for creativity and ideation.

RWRLT   Clearly communicate what success looks like.

RWRLT   Create a culture where failing is okay, and even encouraged, as from failing, we often move forward. When there is a fear of failure, creativity is often stifled.

RWRLT   Support stress management with quiet spaces/times during the day, and in the office, when RWR are onsite, for meditation and reflection.

RWRLT   Share routines that will assist your team to get their day started on the right track. Warning: if you are not an inspirational speaker or known for inspiration, please do not suddenly attempt to get "deep" with your RWRs, instead, consider ways that may be beneficial. This is about sharing routines, not forcing them!

RWRLT   Select mentors to assist and partner with all team members, and not just struggling team members. Focusing on mentoring only when there is an issue makes it seem like a punishment, when in fact, the collaboration and guidance is often instrumental in a RWR's mindset!

RWRLT   Bring in guest speakers or superstars in the industry that have mastered mindset for coaching and inspiration.

RWRLT   Demonstrate how your mindset has positively and negatively impacted you. Be vulnerable here, and at most times, as this is about being transparent and real with the RWR as you build your relationship (and master mindset).

RWRLT   Ask for success stories to be shared on overcoming distractions, disappointments and the doldrums.

Hopefully now you see and feel that mindset is not as mystical as it may have seemed at first.

The plan is that you will now please think of mindset as attitude and outlook combined with actions to progress an idea or project forward.

Mindset matters, and Remote Work Rockstars rock their minds to rock what is assigned!

# Chapter 5:
# Communicating Effectively

*"Keep a team chatroom open. There is nothing more important in a group remote project than casual communication. Not just official emails and work updates, but the ability to sit back and chat."*

*~ David Rabin,*

*Lenovo*

While communication has been mentioned often already, an entire chapter is dedicated to it because communication can, and will, make or break the relationships, and therefore the results, of a remote worker.

Remote Work Rockstars see communication as not one-way or two-way, rather as *every way*, meaning it is about the verbal, written, non-verbal and visual communication...and the timing and perspective on all of it make an impact as well!

For communicating as an off-site contributor, often extra effort is required, meaning your impression on others is based on emails and phone calls along with video representation across a platform of choice. While it may seem like a habit tip, it is placed here in the communicating effectively chapter because time management is essential for Remote Work Rockstar success, as any delayed, even slightly tardy information, reflects as

mismanagement and poor
communication skills…yikes!

For your Remote Work Rockstar
success in the area of communication,
please incorporate the following:

☆ Resist asking "Why" questions and
replace inquiries in all formats as
"What" and "How" questions. This
does not mean you will not get to the
"why" or the reason, as we call it,
rather, "Why" questions create
defensiveness, and "What" and "How"
questions create conversation. In
person, remote, on the phone, or in
emails, replace your tend-to-be-
accusatory "Why" questions with
uplifting "What" and "How"
questions, and watch how the rapport
soars!

☆ Use an Out of Office message and
change your Voicemail greeting each
day. Yes, that is communication, and it
takes time. While not everyone will
read and/or listen, you can establish
your pattern of communication by
including when you will be available,

returning calls, and if there is open time in your schedule that day.

☆ Start your messages, and in particular, your emails, with something other than "I". Using "I" means the communication is about you. Please think about less "I", "Me", "My" to position sincerely for more "You", "Yours", "Ours". For example, a simple change from "I enjoyed meeting you yesterday at the conference" to "What a pleasure it was connecting with you at the conference yesterday!" moves the message from a flat informative sentence to an engaging, moving message!

☆ Stay away from vague language, including "etcetera", "and so on", and "and so forth". This lack of specification can lead to people not trusting your expertise.

☆ Give credit where it is due and/or share in credit. Do not become a pat-myself-on-the-back-er!

☆ Send hand-written notes to people who also work remotely and those at the region or headquarters, clients, customers, suppliers, vendors, contractors, and others who participate in your success. Notes that are handwritten are far more likely to make an impact and be saved more than a text or email ever will be.

☆ Drop the "kind of" "I'll try", and "maybe" comments. Be confident and clear in your communication. Such vague, non-committal, non-value-add words are not those of a confident RWR, and they can diminish people's interest in listening to someone offsite.

☆ Be someone who appropriately promises and appropriately delivers. Notice I did not say over-deliver? One time over delivering, meaning getting something done ahead of time or under budget, and that is a pleasant surprise. Sure, that can be good for relationship-building, and communication is a huge part of that. Still, if you do it repeatedly, people think you are a sand-bagger, and expect the early or under-budget delivery, so if you get in a poorly-serving habit of "over delivering", when you do deliver on time or just inside the budget, people think it's late or over budget. That is when your past can backfire, and in a big way negatively impact your present, and even your future!

☆ Practice your Emotional Intelligence. Think of Emotional Intelligence as "the ability to recognize and assess one's own and other people's emotions, while discriminating among the various emotions and label them appropriately in order to guide perspective and actions as a guide to thinking and behavior". If you are or are not familiar with it, Emotional Intelligence includes a great deal of empathy. Empathy is not sympathy. Empathy is a characteristic of communication that is conveyed when you consider someone else's perspective, how his/her emotions may play out, and attempt to put yourself in their shoes before communicating, acting or suggesting anything.

☆ Know enough about your sense of humor to know not everyone loves your sense of humor. In Chapter 2, it was encouraged that you keep your sense of humor muscles firmed up, and this is not running contrary to that, rather reminding you that not all jokes are universal, and across email or even simple distance, some things, and therefore, some people, are deemed less funny than that may have been on-site.

☆ Assess and share how you like to be coached. Coaches or leaders, tend to only coach the way they like to be coached. Remote Work Rockstars are able to communicate their best learning style so they can learn best.

☆ Stick with the BASICS of communication (remote or not) with the following words to start emails, voicemails, meetings and sessions in order to give the purpose before the ask/tell. BASICS is an example of an acrostic, which is a word puzzle that for each aspect of the puzzle, the first letters combine to form a word. The acrostic BASICS is a reminder to start each sentence with:

*B – Because*
*A –Appreciating/respecting*
*S – Since*
*I – In order to...*
*C – Considering*
S – (Smile: we sense tone!)

The BASICS surely apply to leaders, too. How communication happens, or doesn't happen, perceived, or in reality, has a huge impact on how RWRs feel about their job, their contributions, their loyalty, and the company, overall.

Remote Work Rockstar Leaders level up the communication through all of the tips for the RWRs, and, in addition, include the following:

- **RWRLT** Have weekly check-ins with your team to talk about progress, ideas, and what is happening with them personally, too.
- **RWRLT** Be aware, and yet not overly awkward, about body language. This is an important cue that

something could be wrong and is often left unaddressed.

`RWRLT` Practice communication openly and include training as part of your leadership strategy.

`RWRLT` Train on Emotional Intelligence. This is the #1 reason people don't get promoted or fail at their jobs.

`RWRLT` Role play is dreaded by staff, and yet is one of the most effective ways to practice. challenging conversations.

`RWRLT` Schedule virtual lunch meetings or happy hours without an agenda so the team can spend time getting to know each other.

`RWRLT` Encourage your team to reach out to each other to connect and engage on an ongoing basis.

`RWRLT` Share personal information about yourself to encourage team members to do the same.

`RWRLT` Provide feedback to your team on communication gaps and how to improve them.

**RWRLT** Request feedback from your team members and fellow leaders, and then accept that feedback, meaning:

> **RWRLT** Once you receive the feedback, don't defend it.
> **RWRLT** After you receive feedback, share with the RWRs what you heard and what you are going to do with it.

Much like in the Real Estate market, the thoughts go to "location, location, location", in leadership, and especially in Remote Work Rockstar leadership, it is all about "communication, communication, communication"!

# Chapter 6:
# Meeting Magnetism via Video

*"Rig up a good video setup with nice headphones, a quality microphone, and lighting. And devote blocks of time to video calls. One of the things that emerges from the research is that switching costs are high. If you switch from a physical meeting to email to another email on a different subject to a calendar to a video meeting to another email – every time you switch modes, you waste time. Have dedicated blocks of time for virtual contact and dedicated blocks of time for face-to-face contact."*
*~ Rory Sutherland,*
*Ogilvy*

Video sessions are not calls, they are meetings, or webinars. Calls are on the phone. People get confused, and even blindsided, when someone asks for a call, and then there is video involved. To have meeting magnetism via video, be prepared for video at all times you are working your designated work hours.

Unfortunately, while I was co-facilitating a leadership academy with a client, someone came up behind a participant who was facing the screen and made some rude gestures behind him. People saw it, were rightly offended, and it became a Human Resources discussion that afternoon. Not only was it unprofessional, undignified, and unnecessary, the session was being recorded for participants who could not attend, and it took editing to tweak the video before it could be shared without concern of negative impact. These acts on video conferencing software are often captured, and this is, again, an impression, so put forward your best on any day, regardless of who is in the meeting!

While the list of guiding tips and tools below is long, and a video meeting could be short, keep in mind that the visual part of communication, and the non-verbals are picked up when teleconferencing, so be present, be prepared, and be productive with, and through, the following:

Pre-meeting:
☆ Check your camera for functionality and for a quality picture. If there is a distraction from quality, you may want a virtual background to limit the "look-see-ers" checking out what is happening in your location. (More on virtual backgrounds will be shared later.)
☆ Download the preferred new or updated software well before meeting time.
☆ Register, if required.

☆ Upload a current head shot photo to the site for your muted video still when not using video.

☆ Turn off any overhead fans to avoid the choppiness of sound and sight of the visual breaks in lighting.

☆ Test your microphone for proper sound to avoid saying "Can you hear me?". And, if the audio is choppy before, or during the meeting, make no "noise" about it and quickly mute the speaker and microphone and call in.

☆ Test your camera to make sure it is at/near eye-level and not putting you in a position where you are looking up or down at others, as either way, you look less "normal", and either angle is less flattering.

☆ Be professionally attired in what you would wear if you were onsite for the meeting (covered in Chapter 3).

☆ Log on a minute or two early to check your presenting self (how you look online).

☆ Use a virtual background if you don't like the look of the area behind you. A virtual background can be your company logo, a bookshelf or a plain screen. Resist making it a beach or something/somewhere you would not be for a meeting. These take up less bandwidth, too, so they can be preferred if there are connection/streaming issues. If you are presenting, though, no virtual backgrounds since they "eat" your movements, and you will have people laughing at your "lost" arms rather than listening and watching you present.

☆ Turn off everything else on your device being used (including push notifications from email). Background distractions and noises are noticed by others, even when you believe you are discreet about noticing them!

During the meeting:
☆ Resist looking at yourself, and do not fix your hair! No video session is your next mirror or primping time. And, yes, people can tell when you are looking at yourself. Touching your hair a lot can give the impression that

you are interested in your appearance more than the content.

☆ Remember, people are watching, and use "speaker view" if someone is presenting so that you give full attention to that person and not checking out others in the meeting.

☆ Mute your video during someone else's presentation after you have been on for greetings and/or group discussion, if the presentation is longer than a few minutes.

☆ Mute your audio unless you are speaking.

☆ Mute your video during a meeting or short presentation if/when you get up to get coffee, water, use the facilities.

☆ Use chat for questions, and/or raise your hand on video to be called on so as to not nearly speak through/over someone.

☆ Watch talking over one another, as the audio and video often do not allow for chatter, rather only one person can be heard at any given time.

☆ Keep others in your area out of the screen, including pets and children

By treating each video session as a meeting, you will then act like you would in person in every way possible, from timeliness to eye contact to respectful communication, and agenda following.

If you are presenting via video, here is the etiquette for effective public speaking in a virtual environment:

☆ Send the invitation for a Video Conference, and not a call.

☆ Consider including a video message ahead of time to greet those who register or will be in attendance to show the video and to give them some familiarity with you.

☆ Practice your presentation (not just a review of slides, rather a practice of the delivery fully to be well-versed).

☆ Log in minimally 15 minutes prior to the start and ensure everything is working properly.

☆ Start with a welcome and an open with you on the screen, not a presentation slide, and ensure that first part is not about you and your credentials. Consider asking a question for a reaction or input right away.

☆ Let people know if the session is being recorded.

☆ Encourage people only to acknowledge if they cannot see or hear, rather than asking for confirmation that they can see or hear, and that will save on much noise of getting multiple replies of a "yes" or "no".

☆ Establish and share a goal and state the time frame of the meeting to let people know you are responsible for the time.

☆ Use an agenda of only 2-4 topics to keep the ideas palatable.

☆ Share your screen versus sending deck, and encourage, not demand, people use speaker view during the presentation.

☆ Let people know they can take photos, or use the Snipping Tool to capture information.

☆ Bounce back in for engagement in between agenda topics. Doing this shows great poise and confidence. Plus, the audience or attendees see your face, and you can engage there before moving on with the next section.

☆ Ask questions (and listen to the replies) and/or utilize chat for engagement.

☆ Set up next steps by telling the attendees what will happen following the meeting in regards to notes and assignments.

Remote Work Rockstars look to leaders to be better than them at some things, and handling video meetings successfully is often one of those activities since those events make a product, a brand, a team, and even a company known by the actions of the people invited to participate. Everything above for the RWR applies to the RWR Leaders, and these tips will assist as well:

RWRLT  Encourage your team to stay energized in meetings by including an ice-breaker at the start. A couple options are:

>  RWRLT  Ask for play list recommendations and have the team guess who provided what songs.

>  RWRLT  Start with 10 minutes of connect time or networking for catch-up and getting to know each other.

RWRLT  Bring in trainers to assist with virtual presentations. The focus can then be on the people and content, not technical difficulties.

RWRLT  Use an agenda for guidance and direction. Keep the agenda to 4 or fewer items, and do not include times, so people will stay engaged rather than checking off multiple items and/or watching the clock to see if you are on time.

RWRLT  Practice pausing after each person speaks. This will allow for everyone to be heard without talking over each other.

**RWRLT**   Schedule virtual meetings for less time than in-person meetings. "Zoom Gloom", "Zoom Zap", and Virtual Video Energy Vampires are clever names I've created for what is real…the burnout that comes from little  physical movement and almost no human engagement in the same room while focusing on a screen.

**RWRLT**   If you are compelled to schedule a meeting longer than an hour, have breaks each hour, and consider providing blue light glasses for attendees.

**RWRLT**   Provide presentation and meeting feedback to your Remote Work Rockstars by offering them a chance first to say what they felt went well, then share what you liked about their delivery, followed by what they want to improve, and then what you want them to improve.

Remote Work Rockstar and RWR Leaders know that video sessions require a lot of energy, and different energy than when in person or on the phone, so ensure that throughout meetings, the tone and approach is focused on moving forward and making progress. Flexing your patience muscles will likely be a challenge, and yet by providing the time someone requires to gain confidence and grow, will be the investment in the Remote Work Rockstar she or he deserves!

# Chapter 7:
# Staying Connected

*"To collaborative team members, completing one another is more important than competing with one another."*

*~ John C. Maxwell,*

*Leadership Speaker*

Even though you are a Remote Work Rockstar, you still want to engage with people socially and professionally within your company and outside of your company.

This final chapter is about networking and relating to others fully in ways that have not all been covered in the book previously.

Some ways to do that include:
☆ Have interests outside work.
☆ Create friends and relationships that relate to your passion.
☆ Get a connection you trust to mentor you within work.
☆ Ensure you reach out on professional social media, such as LinkedIn to get connected, stay engaged, and participate in posts and groups.
☆ Secure a coach (professional or otherwise) to assist you in life and business outside of work.
☆ Track your personal goals with others in order to celebrate wins and assess misses or losses.

☆ Send personal notes to thank those who assist you, even if it is for something small.

☆ Compliment others by being willing to let them have the spotlight.

☆ Speak up and give recognition and/or credit to someone who deserves it.

☆ Organize non-work-related events such as a happy hour or other event to stay engaged with those on your team.

☆ Join organizations related to your industry locally, regionally and/or nationally.

☆ Become a part of organizations related to your passion locally, regionally, and/or nationally.

☆ Offer to assist, mentor and/or coach someone else to enhance that person's life.

☆ Be a small (or large) part of creating a new Remote Work Rockstar through your interest and involvement.

Some of the actions a Remote Work Rockstar leader can take are the same those of the RWR. Still, there are additional approaches to staying connected that can be implored, including to:

`RWRLT` Encourage virtual meetings outside of working hours like themed happy hours or book clubs, even if a RWR has some going on also. These need not compete, rather they can work together.

`RWRLT` Have your team members, remote or not, record a video bio to serve as a welcome to each new team member.

`RWRLT` Utilize photos and nicknames to connect the team to one another through familiarizing them with visuals and stories.

`RWRLT` Resist connecting with your RWRs anywhere other than on LinkedIn, as that keeps things professional and does not create awkward moments outside of work.

`RWRLT` Schedule regular check-in calls with your team to invest further in the relationship.

`RWRLT` Send small gifts in the mail to your RWR. to show you are thinking about them. Make sure they relate to their interests, and not imposing your interests on them.

**RWRLT**    Celebrate life events like birthdays, babies, holidays, and weddings with virtual parties.

**RWRLT**    Include co-workers' pets, babies and spouses in casual virtual lunches where you send restaurant delivery or gift cards for everyone to be eating the same food for a similar vibe.

**RWRLT**    Have your team share best practices and expertise as ongoing peer training/coaching.

**RWRLT**    Provide full company virtual updates to keep everyone up to date on policy and changes.

There are so many ways to connect and even more ways to stay connected, so embrace them, rock them, and watch the Rockstars continue to shine!

# Closing Comments

There you have it, ROCKSTAR!

From getting defined as remote work to getting set up, working, and staying connected, you have completed the handbook, the guidebook for your continued success.

Congratulations!

Please use this publication as a reference for your efforts and those following in your footsteps. Remember to encourage others to embrace the approaches, tips and tools to propel them forward in whatever work they are doing.

Here's hoping you were intrigued, inspired, and called to action through the pages you just read in Remote Work Rockstar.

The message of the book is not only that remote workers and team members can be, and are, ROCKSTARS, it is also that being off-site can be an asset and not a disadvantage. Additionally, it is meant to empower the remote worker and the leaders of remote workers to assess and respect what makes us alike as well as different.

Thank you again for being a part of my philosophy and approach to "Reversing the Slobification of America"™ through this book documenting my guidelines for remote work wins and contributions.

Please share your responses and ideas freely. I look forward to your feedback and ideas regarding this publication, anything else you have seen in my other books, on Twitter, Instagram or LinkedIn at @DebbieLundberg, my business Facebook page at https://www.facebook.com/Presenting PowerfullyByDebbieLundberg, and/or on my website at http://www.DebbieLundberg.com.

If you want to get connected directly, Debbie@DebbieLundberg.com or 813.494.4438, are both great avenues for contact.

Additional books you can access on my website include:

- Hey, Where's My Bailout? (co-authored by Todd Josko)
- Lundberg*isms*
- More Lundberg*isms*
- Presenting Powerfully
- Reversing the Slobification of America
- Leading without Losing Your Femininity
- Beyond Networking 101

There, you'll also find ways to book speaking engagements, facilitation and strategy sessions, teaming and training, and/or individual consulting and coaching, plus a new video series, called Leadership Learning, is a virtual program with modules that complement all the writings.

Barb and I continue our The Business of Life Master Class Podcast, and it is available on nearly every platform, too!

With appreciation, thank you again for your investing in you and your life by engaging in the practices in remote work!

As we all move forward in life and in business, remote work will ebb and flow, and the comfort level of it will likely increase. That comfort can become a confidence with the tips and tools implemented from this book.

Remote work, as we know, is not "working from home", and Remote Work Rockstars are not about being the rock of a team or company, solely, and yet they, *you*, can rock your world by being a professionally engaged, dynamic contributor from anywhere as you continue to engage in all you can to enhance your impact on your journey as a ***Remote Work Rockstar***!